INCONSPICUOUS

INCONSPICUOUS
BY RORY GOODE

Copyright 2025

Published by
New Bay Books
Fairhaven, Maryland
NewBayBooks@gmail.com

Cover and Book Design by Rory Goode
agoode1234@outlook.com

A Note on Type:
Display headings are set in Cinzel Decorative;
text is set in Garamond Premier Pro Light

Library of Congress
Cataloging-in-Publication Date
August 2025
ISBN 979-8-9882998-8-2
Printed in the United States of America

First Edition

DEDICATION

For Valerie
my love

&
Audrey and Elaine
my friends

INCONSPICUOUS

A POETRY COLLECTION BY

RORY GOODE

FOREWORD

In creating this collection, I was torn between making its theme purely personal and biographical, or more topical and political. The themes would not be separated. I could not write a poem about myself and my own experience that would not, in all likelihood, be labeled political. Both topics would have to interweave.

I have gathered these poems over the past four or so years of my life, a time in which I was both navigating the first few years of young adulthood and undergoing gender transition.

Through this time I was bothered that I could not find literature I could turn to that encapsulated the complexity of my own experience.

Yes, transitioning was difficult, and the scant amount of literature I did find on the subject repeated that back to me. I did not find literature that investigated the nearly unexplored and undocumented wealth of unique experiences I was undergoing. I wanted to read poetry or fiction that reflected all of the strange intricacies of a shifting identity, of being perceived, of perceiving oneself, of an internal and external division. Not as a tragedy and not sugar-coated either. But instead as a nearly neutral experience, exploring an uncharted territory of self.

I'm sure this book does not encapsulate all of those things, being my first poetry book.

These poems describe real moments in my life, either as narratives or as reflections I had over time. They put you, as I was, in real situations or fictional ones relevant to my own experience. The metaphors that spring from those situations are, like dreams, formed in the language of experience. The metaphors that spring from those situations are, like dreams, formed in the language of unmastered emotion. That's the best language I have to describe the complexity of my transformative experience. To understand them, read the images, not just the words.

You may notice that the style of these poems is often simple, complementing themes of domesticity and everyday experience. This may surprise the reader after expressing my interest in a long list of "strange intricacies." These poems play with themes of complexity and simplicity. They attempt to depict my life as I perceive it. The battle between complexity and simplicity naturally arises from my journey into an "uncharted territory of self." Because an aspect of my existence was at once largely denied, misunderstood or simply unknown, It was my impulse to wonder how I could best explain myself. Should I have been loaded with complicated words like they were ammunition, ready to justify myself as if I were on trial? Or should I try to prove my own normalcy through universal or accessible simplicity? Most importantly, however, I came to wonder why I needed to explain myself in the first place. These poems aim not to explain myself but to explore myself, both in shades of simplicity and complication. You will see that I tend to favor the latter, though at times both modes complement each other and each has its own value.

In some poems, I missed my target of neutrality because I could not remove feelings of pain or frustration inseparable to me from the topic. I hope that this collection, in its simple, expressional and personal style, might nonetheless be a good start in telling the largely unexplored story of gender transition from a personal perspective. It is a privilege to know that the indulgence of telling my own story might be meaningful to someone besides myself. In trying to express and understand myself, I further hope I might express sentiments valuable for you or that help some other understand.

CONTENTS

LITTLE BLUE HERON

People are gathered
At the water's edge
Camera in hand
Just to see him,
The little blue heron,
This afternoon.

And a few women
With children
Are passing and
Not looking.
Among them
She is like a blue poppy
In a crowd of red ones.

She pushes a baby in a white stroller.
Her phone is in her ear
And she speaks
In a nice voice
Like a cello.

And out there sits the little blue heron
on his rock.
Does he have everything he needs out there?
His eyes and head dart with jarring quickness,
But I want to believe this is his leisure.

Does he look up and twitch to spot some predator in the sky,
Or to catch a slipping beam of sunlight
just brushing through the leaves?
Does his long beak lower to watch the water pour over the rocks,
Or to carefully watch for a small swimming thing,
Fearful itself?

But you, Heron,
Give your nosy onlookers no answer
Though they watch and wait
In anticipatory silence.
You bend to the water,
Seductive, like a movie star
Who wishes they would put their cameras away.
When you fly off
the children and women,
Inconspicuous,
Have passed us.
Their laughter fades
As they leave together
And all eyes remain fixed
On the heron's vacant place,

She smiles and thinks
She is so content
To be less interesting
Than a bird,
So relievingly
Inconspicuous.

CHILD

Where was I in the world?
The answer was easy.
I was at work,
In the kitchen, at the sink.
But where in the imposing
And uncharitable expanse
Of the whole world?

My brain ached.
To someone I am nothing.
To me I am everything.
The world inside me is a world itself,
And another exists in every other.
Maybe we all know that,
But cruelty is to pretend that world is no world,
I guessed.

And I broke the dishwasher.
Did it even matter?
It seemed like a very small thing.
The owner, her husband
And their children came in.
He was a big man with a beard.
He was taller than I'll ever be.
He grunted and asked who did the dishes.
I said it was me.

I stood like a useless child,
Feeling soft and pale,
And thought I ought to learn to do something like that.
Like fixing a dishwasher.

When I apologized to the owner.
She told me not to worry,
Though I didn't believe her,
Repeating that I was sorry.

She sent the boys to help clean
Though one quickly returned, asking
"Can I be done now Mom?"
To which she smiled and said "no, "
Reminding him he simply had to,
And that there would be no negotiation.

So boy furrowed his brows up at her,
And shook the brown curls
On his little white head.
"Leave me alone! I don't wanna!" he said
Through pursed lips
Stomping the feet at the ends of his
White toothpick legs.

Leave me alone. I don't wanna.
What a gratifying thing that was to say.

SOMEWHERE I AM A WARM CHIMNEY FOR AN UGLY BLACK BIRD

Somewhere I am a warm chimney for an ugly black bird.
It must be true; boys' eyes slip away like fish
In a little reflective pool,
Sliding out of my hands.

I watched this morning as the small birds sat on the branches.
Winter is each time a womb waiting for spring.
A bird is frantic. Have you watched them turn their heads?
I think of bugs.
Watching an ant move after it's been smashed into the rug.
I think of the mouse in the cupboard,
So timid and greedy.

What hides behind softness and eats what it likes?
So timidly?
What is round and warm?
The feeling of a mammal.

MODESTY IN THE NATIONAL GALLERY

I

IN ESSENCE

I saw some impression of eyes fixed elsewhere,
Or a face briefly in profile
That is untethered now.

We made
Something out of this alone.
We made it in small rooms and in soft voices,
Something intricate,
Nearly rational.

How sad to see it failing,
The image fading,
And so much left missing.

II
THE HALLS OF THE MUSEUM

So strange that I feel in myself something like Adam.
Each twinge, each stroke,
Primordial for us all,
Yet just springing up for me.

Somehow for all that
My companion remains a mystery.
We may be looking at the same painting,
But I am feeling it with an unknowable wailing in me.
And I cannot hear yours,
Whatever it may be,
Whether it wails or sings or hums
In silence.

Other companions, at random, I know
With evidence,
With art.
I conjecture
Then we conjecture.
You tell me what you think
And I fill in the rest
Wherever I see any emptiness.

And others are wordless.
I am putting together the curve of an arm
The squint of an eye
The neck gesturing

III
A FRIEND

There is a portrait of a lady in this museum.
Her face is round. Her cheeks are flushed.
There is sweetness in her eyes like jelly,
Malleable.

How I wish you were here!
You know what things were like then.
You remember
How we were sent howling halfway to hell
On the green grass.
That was good.

I amuse myself.
I indulge myself.
I see an image of you as one of these ladies in this museum
Dressed in one of those dresses with the skirt billowing and the
Corset tight.

I can see you now looking down on me,
Frail, big-nosed, smirking,
Obstinate as ever.
A lady, nevertheless.

WHAT AM I?

What am I?
Words upon words could answer the question
But they are gone in moments
If I can make myself briefly believe
That nothing else exists
Besides the sound of a ticking clock
Or the sight of a raindrop.

I have sleepwalked through
Stores and streets
As if these places were a dull limbo
Between the question and the answer.

I thought to myself,
As I raced around,
That I once did not feel like myself.
Yet this was before I created myself.
Did I spring up out of nowhere?
Someone decided who I would be.
Who was it?

I have looked to others for answers.
I have compared and contrasted
Myself against them.
I have imagined
What another set of eyes sees
And what they see in me.
But I learned nothing.
I only imagined.

As in all of these endeavors
I have been unsuccessful.
I am now accustomed
To forget the question
For the sake of better things.
Like ticking clocks in
My ears
Or raindrops before
My eyes

TO A SPIDER

This morning a small spider
Traveled down her invisible web
Above my sink full of dishes.
Why was I so hesitant to stand beneath her
When I could have quickly crushed her between my hands?

Though I briefly thought to take her life
I moved her with a ladle.
For what reason could I believe her life was
Worth anything less than mine?

I could not believe it
on the grounds of smallness:
To some creatures I am just as small.
I could not claim she was any threat to me,
Though I may shudder at her harmless and spindly appearance.
And though she may not speak or read
I cannot spin a web.

I could have been a spider too
My life is just as delicate.
But I also know,
Like me, she is no stranger to murder
And relishes the taste of a fly.

NATURE IS A FEELING

I

I thought I knew something about it
Descending into the hazy woods
On that purple evening.
Seeing the yellow grass fade to blue
Against green pines.
I loved metaphors more than anything at that age.
The sky was a lady's purple gown.
The stars were crystals in the deep cold earth.
The trees whispered.
The woods danced.
Nature is beautiful,
I thought.

At summer camp I learned that
I had never really seen the stars before.
I was a victim, they said, of
Cars and ugly white streetlights.
All was lost to
towns, streets and factories.
I was certain then, at twelve,
I was on the cusp of knowing almost everything
And that I had discovered the most profound revelation;
Everyone must return.

Where? I guessed it was to nature,
And when? Somewhere way back,
Some older time,
Some better time.
The impression struck me as I
Watched firelight rest gently
On the cheeks of my peers.
There the woods were so black,
The unknown made room
For any fabrication I dared
To imagine existed outside of me.

II

However, a few years later
I had fallen out of love with nature.
Deep green ivy grew up the side of the house
Forever snaking
And regrowing
Where no one needed it.
It wrapped, squeezed and consumed
Like a boa constrictor.
The house was a body
Sinking into the earth.

I watched as my father,
Wiping sweat from his brow,
Wrestled the overgrowth.
As if a tiny pair of shears
Could have saved
That poor house.

Why not sink?
Why not sleep?
Did it matter if shears cut
Ugly green vines
Or soft white wool?

III

A few years later I met Socrates.
Nature is beautiful
His odd round face
split those words in twos
And fourths
And eighths
Into dust
Into nothing.

Nature
It could not be the physical object, not the tree or the branch itself. These come
about through that name. But that tells me nothing about what it is in itself
or where it came from. Is it a force that brings them into being? So what is its
origin? Something deciding? Or is there no reason at all?

Beautiful
A girl, a flower, a sunset. What do they share? Maybe a girl is necessary. But a
sunset? A flower? And necessity is nothing. Dinner is nice, not beautiful, unless
there is some special sentiment or you are starving.

So rushing over red brick
And among white pillars
I tried to forget about
Nature as an
Enemy or
A friend
Or a snake
Or a crystal.

IV

A few years after that
I had no answers left
And my brain carried on
Like a never ending song
I was tired of hearing.

If we must return, what time will we return to? Am I natural?
If I am not natural, am I light pollution? Am I art?
Does it matter if I feel it? Does it matter if I can prove it?

I was surprised to see
It was not so hard
To turn it off,
If only for a moment.

In the courtyard there were no words,
But I heard the sound of bugs and birds
with cars and planes.
There were bushes and benches with
Grass and sidewalk and
Above my head was
a bright budding tree.
Its branches curled upward and dipped in the wind
and its bright white buds were so numerous
I wondered if they felt heavy.
But there was no sign of fatigue or concern
In those winding branches that composed
One bulbous frame
Like a snowglobe.

I thought the tree was beautiful
But I didn't say a word.
Why start a conversation with someone who doesn't speak?

I DON'T KNOW ANY TRANS PERSON IN MY LIFE WHO EVEN PLAYS A SPORT

I don't know any trans person in my life who even plays a sport.
Why does it matter? Who cares?
I never liked to play sports.
No one is putting me or anyone I personally know out.

I feel too frozen for it.
Not cold, just stiff
And quiet
Like I'm tight around the throat.

I can't dance either.
I shudder thinking about it.
Sometimes I think maybe I will in the future.
Later, just not now.

And I don't like new places
Or new people
Or anything unpredictable.

I like a few people I could count on my hand.
I guess because they know me well
And I know none of us play sports.

I guess I just don't like to be seen moving.
And I don't like teams because
I don't like big groups
Because I don't like most people.

I don't *hate* most people
But think I like to keep to myself
Because I'm not sure
I know how to speak a universal language
Or rather transmit a universal signal
By which you could guess half of who I am
Or how to talk to me.

Sometimes I get a little tense or
A little restless
Like I've got to move
Or I've got to speak
And it comes out like a
Cacophonous whirlwind.

I remember the first time it happened
It was like a cork blowing off a champagne bottle.
That was my first love.

The last time I played basketball
I threw a ball in the wrong goal.
The last time I danced I did the move backward
And pulled my partner and I into a pretzel.

But my first love could have poured out smoothly
Instead of blasting off
Or with practice I could have learned those things.
I just didn't do it when I was younger.
I already didn't want to
Because I didn't like teams
Because I didn't like big groups and
Because I didn't like most people.

I didn't *hate* most people.
I just didn't know if
I knew how to speak a universal language

Or if I transmitted a universal signal
By which other kids could guess
Half of who I am
Or how to talk to me.

I guess that's why *I* never liked to play sports
And maybe that's also why
I don't know any trans person in my life who even plays a sport.

DRUNK AT THE BUDDHA IN BOSTON

Finally I am free. There is only here.
The MFA, near empty,
Nine at night
Is a hidden place
At the back of the brain
Like home
Or at least
A long awaited stop
On an endless voyage.

My self is like a dream self
And when my thoughts stir to wake me
I set the aside.
I don't know I am sleeping
And there is nothing else in the world.

I have been looking for something.
It was not lofty Juno.
She was beautiful, but not her own.
Her head had been severed,
Her maimed body was a muse's,
As I gazed upward at her formidable frame
I thought only of the excessive woman
Who for so long (so the plaque read)
Held the goddess captive in her garden
Rendering her a
Frankensteined and forgotten goddess.

It was not Christ
Who had lost his cross and hung eternally
Discolored, bloated, and with his ribs exposed.
Though merely wood
He was shrunken and dry like a
Once living thing.
He had been carved away at
For a thousand years,
Each time more purposefully gruesome.
He was an invention of thousands
Most horrified anticipations,
And his deadly silence evoked the sound of a
Hushed and frightened whisper.

The golden Buddha
Is nothing but himself
And nothing but his own.
He does not command my respect but
Invites me to stop
And join him.
It is only natural
That I respect him.
It is not a question.

His eyes rest
Like the easiest thing in the world,
Like breathing,
And I feel as if I
Can feel him breathe
As I breathe
And we breathe together.

His lips curl
As if he's heard a joke
But at once
Like a patient mother
Who watches a child tumble
As he takes his first steps.

For some time there is silence
A refreshing relieving silence

And a feeling like I am
Ten years old
And there is snow everywhere
And no one is going anywhere.

My self is not a dream self.
There is no sleeping,
Everything has been a dream.
And nothing is *like* home.
I am home
And can always return.

NORMAL

How could that be true
When I've seen it with my own eyes?
I know what it is like in the room
On a tired afternoon
And you're there
And everything is normal.

Yes, *normal*
I swear it's all normal.
I could prove it's normal.
The memory of meeting your eyes for the first time
Or you, maybe that same afternoon,
Disquieted, folding laundry.

Maybe I left a dirty mug on the on the counter
And maybe I'm pushing the guilty thought aside because
That's what boyfriends do
And it's all very normal.

No, maybe it's better than normal.
I think "that's what boyfriends do."
And I'm a little happy.
It's simple and smooth
And fits into place.

Neither of us is mistaken.
There's no other thing
That never was
Or should have been.
There's only now and
It's just normal.

CREPE MYRTLE

Though you live
Among the brick
In a little square box,
I know you don't feel like a captive.

We cannot make a dancer dance.
Otherwise the dance is stiff and spoiled.
Like a dancer, Crepe Myrtle, you are
Nothing but yourself.
For only two weeks I saw you
Perform in sultry pink.

You laughed so lightly and effortlessly
For such a stubborn unmovable thing.
You looked upward as you did the whole routine
And the brick box beneath you was nothing.

So while you retreat back into
Deep hidden green
I will not pay any mind to your absence.
There is not beauty in your vibrance
Without your bold defiance.

THE WORST DAY OF THE WHOLE SUMMER

It was the worst day of the whole summer.
Every common thing like
Working, cooking, or eating
had gone excessively wrong
And I hated to be reminded
That the whole impractical plan
Of our whole lives

Never made any sense.
You knew that and
I knew that
And we never said it once.
But the cat was out of the bag.
We were idiots.

I saw every obstacle and defiantly
Leapt forward.
How stupid could I possibly be
To run toward inconvenience
And complication
As if blindly stepping into fire?

I felt like a silly little kid
Digging for pennies to buy
Something he does not understand the price of
And cannot afford.

Our pennies didn't even buy us
Games or toys or excitement.
No, just dinner and soap.
The same dinner that had to be
Made every night
Again and again.
But we cooked it the same.
We took turns and
Made plans
About who would do what
And when.

We made sure everything
Was fair and even
And careful and thoughtful
As we set the table and
went to all the trouble
Just to sit down and
Eat together.

UNITY IN THE NATIONAL GALLERY

I

I see the image
Of a face
Now in portrait.

It is my own face and
Though the image appears static,
I know it is only slow moving
Like the big hand of a clock.
I know this face
Is only a welcomed guest.

Only a few things remain constant:
Eyes, ears, mouth and nose.
But there is no trace of me.

II

I am washed away by the undertow of the world.
Should I despair?
If "I" am washed away
What is left?

A statue is conceived
In the human brain
And eternally wears
The same face.

Should I believe this security
Is worth sacrificing
the freedom of motion?

III

Only a few things remain constant:
Eyes, ears, mouth and nose.
If this is so how do I know
I am not you?

I am not me from yesterday
I am not me from tomorrow.
As much as I
Am not you.

And if by chance
I was me from yesterday
Or am still me tomorrow
I may as well
Be you
And you may as well
Be me.

TO A SUNSET

Coming toward you is like getting there finally.
It's funny how I thought there would be so much harder
Or so much farther.
But no, I found you practically right outside the door
Where you always are
I just didn't know you were *there*.

I could blush the smallest morsel of
The same colors you show me.
No thought, no word of mine is worth
What you are.
I leave myself as if I am
A pair of shoes at your door.

You are red, a little pink, and a little hazy in your summer heat
As a branch sways above my head
And a loud cicada cries out for love.
You are transforming the water
As you darken the tall grass.
As if it were blinking.
As if it were breathing.

I CANNOT SLEEP

I cannot sleep.
A small fan doesn't do much
In a tiny room at the bottom of a boat.

On a boat of all places?
How could any of that follow me
On a boat so far away from home?

And how could I think
In this claustrophobic heat
Of snow?

A snow where nothing grows,
That kind of snow.
Nothing like a downy Christmas eve.
Winter was months ago
But still I think of snow.

I see that I am on this boat
And you are here
And now is now,
But I see snowflakes in my mind

And feel, briefly, as if nothing has changed.
Maybe I should wake you
But I don't.
How could I explain?
The black blue water
Just barely visible
Is just enough
For me to know that
Now is now.

I could laugh.
I am like a dog
Who doesn't know
He's not a puppy.

ABOUT THE AUTHOR

Being a child on Hanover street encouraged an interest in history and a love of speculation. Every building had already lived at least three lives. Like most children, I loved to ask my parents questions. I often asked questions about the architecture of the street or of our over one-hundred-year-old house. Usually these questions couldn't be answered without touching upon the house's Lazarus-like history. For example, I never understood why our bathroom had a small attachment on the side, not large enough to be a useful room, but too open to be a closet. Or why our dining room was so useless. It was too big to be a dining room alone, but too transitory and open to be a living room. So it remained a large and useless space with a table and chairs that no one ever sat on. These rooms were not intended to be bathrooms or dining rooms. They were built before bathrooms existed. Unfortunately I don't remember every explanation my parents gave for each oddity of our house. I only remember that there was always a historical explanation. The past was an integral part of the present and was therefore also an integral part of my imagination.

I often remedied my childlike confusion with historical explanations, though I was usually mistaken. For example, between the ages of three and five I misheard adults saying the phrase "next door" and thought they were instead saying "next store." This, I thought, made perfect sense because perhaps in the past it was necessary for each household to have its own business and for the family to live upstairs. Though I imagined that this practice had since become unnecessary, the phrase "next store" must have stuck as a colloquialism. I didn't know why the practice was once common or necessary because I didn't think through the explanation that far. I am sure that I dismissed this theory soon after I learned how to read.

There was plenty within walking distance to entertain a little kid, though nothing was without a story or entirely conventional. I had the privilege of being one small walk and a right turn away from a movie theater. This movie theater, however, was in no way average. It had a history, not just as a very old movie theater, but as a theater with actors and without screens. Overhead inside the theater, they had closed off some of those luxurious old fashioned box seats that had become unsafe to stand on. I was never scared stepping into the old-smelling darkness of the ancient theater before the movie was on. But there was a haunted and intriguing energy in the room that made seeing any movie there much more exciting than seeing a movie anywhere else.

Though I was nearly certain at that age that ghosts were real, none of these things, whether it was ghosts or old creaky buildings, frightened me that much. The presence of ghosts seemed common and nearly unavoidable. And within the four to six years I had been alive, no ghost had ever deliberately frightened or hurt me, so there was nothing to worry about. I always felt sort of bad for the ghosts. I imagined that it must have been pretty uncomfortable to watch someone move into and live in your own house. It must have been lonely to live unseen, unheard and forgotten. So I tried my best to remain compassionate.

Up the street, at the top of the hill, there was a playground next to a large graveyard. I don't know why, but often after play time I would walk through it with my parents while looking at the headstones. Once I learned to read I took great interest in the names and stories on the graves and plaques. I remember one of these walks as the first time I thought seriously about death. One day I had wandered off through the headstones and was far off from my parents. I discovered a large headstone with three small colorful teddy bears on it. Being a child and attracted to the colorful bears, I was curious about the headstone and stepped closer to it. There was an unusual amount of writing on it explaining that the grave belonged to three children who had died tragically in a fire. As I read I pictured the macabre incident vividly.

The futility of offering a toy to a dead child, especially after I had the careless impulse to follow the bears myself, moved me to tears that I couldn't control. I stopped them and dried them as quickly as I could. I didn't want to explain what I had seen to my parents. I was worried they might decide I wasn't grown up enough to walk through the graveyard, and I didn't want to lose that privilege.

Though that town, Glen Rock, made it impossible to ignore the presence of the dead, I don't mean to give the impression that it wasn't a lively or happy place. Some places, in fact, were too alive. An old burned-down and graffitied-factory, a lair to many wild cats, guarded the walking trail I frequented with my siblings. Weeds and cats, little untameable signs of life, bursted from up out of the ground and clung to the factory's skeleton. It was a lively tradition that each year in the middle of the night on Christmas Eve, carolers in historically accurate costumes paraded down my street loudly singing. I was no stranger to loud noises in the middle of the night, living directly across from the old fashioned red brick fire department. I was sometimes startled awake by the sound of the blaring sirens and the bright red lights. In our backyard there was a pine tree that stood taller than our house. Spring time was always especially beautiful. Though the pine tree was the tallest, I had decided that the light pink dogwood tree in the corner of the yard was my favorite. It always blossomed just in time for my birthday at the end of May. This made me feel like the tree was my tree, and that it blossomed for me.

That town and the house I lived in there was the setting of my earliest and sometimes happiest childhood memories. It feels impossible to recount every peculiar thing about those years or every significant moment within a short biographical essay. "The Old House" has always had sort of a mythical quality about it. I was around eight years old when we moved out, and it still exists in my mind from an eight year old perspective. I have visited the area since, but it is hard to tell what changes are true objective changes to the town and which things reflect changes in me. I know that there has been some objective decline. Many of the small businesses that existed there, such as the movie theater, have since been shut down. When I lived in that house it was painted a pastel baby blue color that has been replaced with a dull shade of brown. I have seen pictures online of the kitchen, once covered in retro mint tiles, redone in a cheap looking black and white modern design.

My younger brother just barely remembers the house and our sister, younger than both of us, does not remember much of it at all. Only my brother and I share these odd memories and refer to the mythical place called "The Old House." That elusive happy, pretty place filled with dust and ghosts, at once comforting and idyllic but haunted and strange.

I sometimes think it is the birthplace of my imagination. There is something childlike and primitive in me that longs to return to these same feelings and images as if finding them again might make me whole.

I cannot fully romanticize that place and time. No time or place is ever perfect, no matter how novel or idyllic. However, I nevertheless get an impression of "The Old House" as an Eden that I fell out of. Maybe we all feel that way about growing up, but having a place to assign as Eden makes the impression especially vivid. When we moved away I was surprised to see that there were not old and storied houses everywhere. The houses in the town we moved to were uniform and cube shaped in most places. It seemed like reality took on a new filter. Life no longer had the same dreamlike quality. Things became sharper and clearer though uglier.

As everyone does, I grew older and ate the fruit from the tree of knowledge. I did have happy times, especially when I was alone reading or playing guitar. I have fond memories of going to summer camp for a few years where I happily spent almost a full week outside. But with growing older and losing innocence comes complexity, both for better and for worse. I have overcome many difficult things in my life and I am proud of my own resilience. But I don't want to burden the reader with a long list of adversities. Perhaps some of those stories might be interesting, but I'm personally tired of reviewing them.

I will however touch upon the theme of gender identity as I have promised to in this book. In adolescence we all go through a process of exploring and acquiring a new sense of identity. It's a natural part of the ugly curse that is eating the fruit. Our brains become filled with more and more "stuff." By that I mean more words, more ideas, more beliefs, and naturally more "me" and "you" and "us" and "them." We all seek to define ourselves and create a sense of identity. It is a natural and necessary part of life both for good and for ill.

I remember when I was a teenager first working through my own feelings on the subject, trying to explain that I was not happy with the gender I was assigned at birth, I would often receive responses from well meaning adults along the lines of "why does it matter what your label is? Are you not just a person? Why does your gender define you?" It sounded like a good argument. Why did it matter so much? How could something that seemed so arbitrary create so much distress for me?

After all, gender is mostly superficial and arbitrary, right? It only describes how you look on the outside, doesn't it? Isn't it what's inside that counts? This all sounds fine—but there is a problem. What is outside? What is inside? How do I know what is outside and inside? Where does the body end and the mind begin? And furthermore, if gender were not such a big deal, why does the topic incite so much controversy, fear and anger?

Trans people have some of the most thoughtful and beautiful relationships with themselves, with life, and with reality. It is hard to walk down the path that many of us take without asking some hard questions. I cannot speak for every trans person, but I felt like reality split open when I became aware of the necessity of transition. The realization that my outside did not match my inside in a fundamental way forced me to re-examine almost everything. We consider gender to be such a fixed and defining characteristic of identity that we are surprised and confused to see it change. At worst we are suspicious. In a time when I understood myself less I had internalized these sentiments and was suspicious of myself. How could the child at the beginning of this essay, who took no issue with wearing frilly pink dresses, be unable to grow into a young woman? How could that child be the same person? The identity that I needed to grow into was not meaningless or arbitrary. Our external identities do matter. I had experienced enough serious discomfort living as an identity that I was unhappy with to know that it mattered. At the same time, my transition opened my awareness to how fluid external identity is. Though fluid does not mean arbitrary, the fluidity of things reminds us of their ephemerality. Everything in life is changing and fleeting. Gender and identity itself are no different. The argument "why does it matter what your label is? Why does your gender have to define you?" is a mistaken one. Though it may be in some sense "what's on the inside that counts" and our labels may be at times arbitrary, our sense of self is a fundamental part of our humanity.

It is not vain or confused for a person to feel beautiful in a dress, or strong and athletic in his body, or intelligent or capable or any of these things. Asking this question about gender is the same as asking why anyone does any of these things. It's like asking "why must you dress up to go out? Isn't it what's on the inside that counts? Why must you feel beautiful? Why does that label matter?" We are not beautiful or strong forever. It is not everything we are. But we also should not deny ourselves the happiness of wearing a face that satisfies us. Trans people are more aware than anyone of the ephemeral nature of our identities. A better question to ask in response to the "why does it matter so much" inquiry is to ask instead "why does it matter if it changes?"

I spoke earlier of a beautiful depth with which trans people understand themselves and the world. I don't believe this depth comes innately with transition, as if being trans were either elusively powerful or incredibly difficult on its own. Instead, this intelligent understanding of ourselves is a natural consequence of our courage. It is the outside world that projects its own confusion and suspicion onto us. Many of us are already struggling to define ourselves as we try to relate our identities to the outside world. It took me years to realize that if it were not for the scrutiny that trans people receive, I may never have had to philosophically ruminate on these questions to try to justify myself. It seems almost as ridiculous to me now as trying to psychologically and philosophically dissect yourself to understand why you like to wear the color blue.

Asking these questions has made me a thoughtful person, but I also recognize how these questions have in the past led to an unnecessary sense of isolation from myself and from others. I saw myself as too divergent. I saw the person I was becoming as too disconnected from the person I once was. Again, how could that child who took no issue with wearing frilly pink dresses grow up to become a man? The answer is not that complicated. I simply wanted to.

In trying to understand myself I unknowingly sought to justify myself. I separated myself from the intimate early childhood I described at the beginning of this essay, as if to prove my sense of identity it was something I needed to despise and abandon. I falsely imagined that something must have gone wrong, or that I had altered the natural course of my life. I felt like my child self was a separate person and that those happy and vivid memories didn't belong to me. I wasn't able to see that these thoughts reflected nothing more than internalized transphobia.

Trans people are unique and beautiful for our courage. But in most other ways there is not much that separates us from anyone else. All human beings fall out of Eden. Our brains become filled with more words, ideas and beliefs. More "me" and "you," more "us" and "them." We learn to live with contradictions. We develop an identity and appearance that is ever changing and brings us both happiness and suffering. We must accept that we cannot do away with it, but it is also not everything we are. There are times in life where we all must choose between our own happiness and the approval of others. These experiences are universal.

That is why meditative simplicity is a major theme in this poetry book. I see simplicity as a profound form of liberation. Sometimes we think we need power to find liberation, and we look for power in the wrong places. We imagine that if we are thorough and intelligent enough to justify ourselves, perhaps we will free ourselves. Or perhaps if we fight tirelessly we will win our own liberation. There are good, noble and necessary fights to take on in the world, but we do not need to live with the projected voices of our opponents in our minds in an effort to remain vigilant.

It is good to ask hard questions. To ask what nature is, to ask what an identity is, to ask why you are the way you are or how you got there. But sometimes we have to lay these things down, even if only for a while, and look at the reflection on the water, or the swift movement of a squirrel outside the window or an odd cloud in the sky. We have to seek liberation not only externally or politically, but within ourselves and our own lives. We must give ourselves the liberty of peace. Not every contradiction or difference between our present self and our past self is a problem to be solved. Both simply are. There is no other life I could have lived, and no other person I could have been. There is only this life. I am still the same child that lived in that baby blue Victorian house— and I am not that child at all.